101 COOL THINGS TO DO IN ROBLOX

Published in 2022 by Mortimer Children's
Books Limited
Part of Welbeck Publishing Group Limited
20 Mortimer Street, London W1T 3JW

The publishers would like to thank the
following sources for their kind permission to
reproduce the pictures in this book.
SHUTTERSTOCK: /Kundra: 4, 8, 14, 20, 26, 30,
36, 42, 46, 52, 58, 66, 72, 78; /Christian
Bertrand: 33; /SkillUp: 2, 12, 18, 24, 34, 40,
48, 54, 60, 64, 70, 76.

All game information correct as of July 2021.

A CIP catalogue record for this book is
available from the British Library.

ISBN: 978 1 83935 133 4

Printed in Dongguan, China

1 3 5 7 9 10 8 6 4 2

FSC
www.fsc.org
MIX
Paper from
responsible sources
FSC® C144853

Author: Kevin Pettman
Design: Dynamo Limited
Design Manager: Sam James
Editorial Manager: Joff Brown
Production: Melanie Robertson

101 COOL THINGS TO DO IN ROBLOX

MORTIMER

CONTENTS

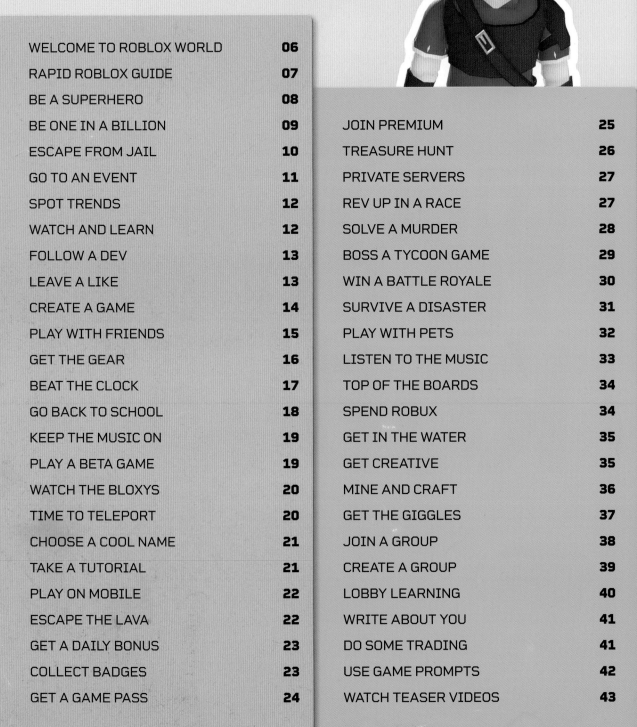

WELCOME TO THE ROBLOX WORLD!

It's no surprise that you love ROBLOX, because millions of other players do too! With thousands of awesome games and a unique universe to explore, including linking up with friends and customising your character, there's no end to the fun you can have. This brilliant book reveals over 100 of the coolest ROBLOX things to do, so get ready for an epic ride around the ROBLOX world!

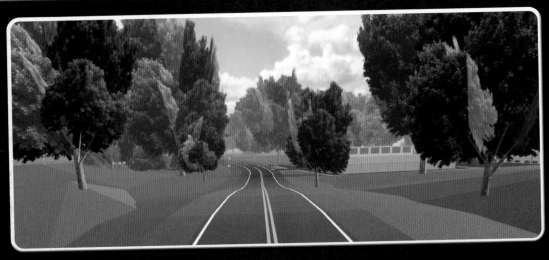

DRIVING EMPIRE

STAYING SAFE ONLINE

ROBLOX is a free online game where players choose from a huge selection of activity games. Users set up their character profile and control that character in games. ROBLOX users can 'chat' through the text feature, which can be restricted to friend-only chat or switched off. Chat has a filter and moderation system and users aged 12 and under can only communicate with gamers they accept as friends. Parents and adults can find out more information at corp.roblox.com/parents.

RAPID ROBLOX GUIDE

Time to speed through a quick-fire guide to ROBLOX and discover the important stuff to know about the world's best game.

ROBLOX can be downloaded to a tablet, mobile, Xbox console or computer, with internet access needed to play. You must give your character, called an avatar, a unique name and a look. Pick from fashion and hair accessories to skin tones and body types.

Long Pastel Hair
By Roblox

Price	◆ 100	**Buy**
Type	Accessory | Hair	
Genres	**Town and City**	
Description	So fun and free!	

Try On 2D

☆ 30K

Games range from action and adventure journeys to puzzles, races, obstacle courses, simulators, roleplaying, building, superheroes and many more. All the games are created by other ROBLOX users. With the Studio tool you can even build your own games!

FUN FACT!
ROBLOX has around 150 million users each month, and developers – the people who make games – are together paid over £200 million each year!

During a game you can check the settings so that you know how to move your character and what your graphics quality, camera sensitivity and other settings are. This can help improve your play and game skills. Access this through the menu button on screen or on the Xbox controller if you're a console player.

Most games are free, but some need the in-game currency, called Robux. Having Robux to spend also means players can buy more cosmetics for their character and get special access in some games. Roblox Premium is a paid subscription with other benefits too.

① BE A SUPERHERO

Capes and suits at the ready – it's time to become a superhero and save the day! Loads of ROBLOX games feature masked heroes, like Batman and Spider-Man, and let you zoom around in disguise and beat the baddies.

If you want some help getting ready for a superhero scrap, then try a training game or simulator. Super Power Training Simulator is a game that gets you fighting, running and thinking like a masked master, with lots of incentives to boost your talents.

Missions can include rescuing victims, reaching new levels, unlocking weapons and collecting coins. In-game maps can lead you to your target, and teaming up with other powerful superheroes is often the way to crack each quest.

AGE OF HEROES

TOP TIP!
Make sure that your abilities match your mission. In Heroes of Robloxia, your super power can be switched between strength, speed, telekinesis, electricity and plasma.

GAMES TO PLAY
- MAD CITY
- SUPER HERO LIFE II
- SUPER HERO TYCOON
- AGE OF HEROES

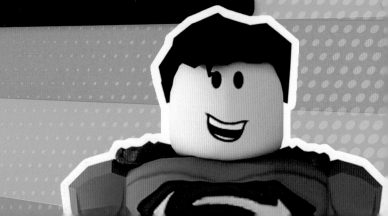

BE ONE IN A BILLION

The elite ROBLOX games have been visited billions of times, so don't miss out on seeing what all the fuss is about for yourself.

The reason these titles are so hugely popular is because they are well made with lots of features, options and extras to keep gamers coming back. Because of the size of these billionaire beasts, the servers can be larger than those of a regular game – MeepCity has a server size of 200 users, which makes for hectic action! Look out for spinoffs and similar games to these popular titles. The official games are likely to be good, but games made by other developers are often rubbish! The series of Piggy games, including Piggy and Piggy (BOOK 2), have a billion plus visits, but just 100 players can play at a time.

ADOPT ME!

22 MILLION VISITS!

By May 2021, Adopt Me! had 22 billion visits – a ROBLOX record!

GAMES TO PLAY

- ADOPT ME!
- MEEPCITY
- ROYALE HIGH
- WORK AT A PIZZA PLACE

3 ESCAPE FROM JAIL

Want to see what life is like behind bars? Well, get your prison gear on (usually a bright orange jumpsuit!) and act like a criminal trying to break free.

It's never an easy task, as guards or police officers will be on your case, ready to round you up and send you back to your cell. Busting out from jail requires planning, bravery, weapons and plenty of sneaking around without being seen by officers or CCTV cameras. If being a criminal all gets too much for you, there's usually the option to switch sides. Before a game starts you can choose to be a prisoner, a guard or a cop. Choosing to be a different role can develop your skills and escape tactics for the next time you're a bad guy!

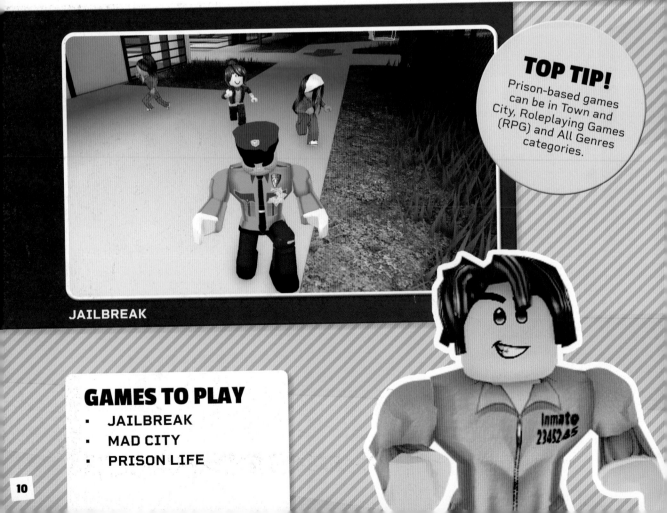

JAILBREAK

TOP TIP!
Prison-based games can be in Town and City, Roleplaying Games (RPG) and All Genres categories.

GAMES TO PLAY

- JAILBREAK
- MAD CITY
- PRISON LIFE

4 GO TO AN EVENT

Not all of the super cool things to do in the ROBLOX universe involve playing a game directly.

Some of the best non-gaming examples are Events, which ROBLOX holds all the time. Under the main menu options on screen, current Events to visit are always clearly labelled. These could include tie-ins with epic new movies, TV shows, award ceremonies, sporting events and holiday season content. Click on it to be whisked away to another exciting digital world. Events could offer you exclusive avatar clothing and emotes, unlocked items, badges and access to limited time shows. ROBLOX has frequently teamed up with Star Wars, including fun challenges and offering themed rewards for lucky players who get involved.

LIVE EVENT: IN THE HEIGHTS BLOCK PARTY

1 MILLION VISITS!

A ROBLOX event for the popular *Ready Player Two* sci-fi book had over one million users visit in the first 24 hours.

In the Heights
Block Party
By Roblox Arena Events

Favorite   Follow   28K+

5 SPOT TRENDS

If something is popular with you and your friends, you can be pretty sure there's already a ROBLOX game about it! If there's a new film out or a craze for a videogame, try looking for it in the Games search bar. Keeping up with new trends and spotting what's hot in ROBLOX means you'll be among the first to try the latest stuff.

6 WATCH AND LEARN

MURDER MYSTERY 2

The 'spectate' function in some games is a clever way to boost your success. So, if you are eliminated but can carry on watching the action unfold, or even shadow the person who killed or beat you, then do so! You can see what moves they make and pick up winning tips. You don't always need to have been eliminated, either – at the start, you may have the option of just watching others play.

Watch and learn – you can try out these moves in your next game.

GAMES TO PLAY
- MURDER MYSTERY 2
- SURVIVOR

7 FOLLOW A DEV

'Dev' means developer. These are the people or groups who build and update each ROBLOX game. On each game's homepage it will say who the dev is – click or tap on this to discover more details about them. You could find more info about the game and dev, some frequently asked questions (FAQs) and any other ROBLOX games that the dev has created. So dive in for dev details!

[UPDATE 14]
Blox Fruits
By **Go play eclipsis**

This is the 'dev'.

Favorite   Follow   733K+   54k+

BLOX FRUITS

FUN FACT!
Devs often release special in-game codes to their fans to help them enjoy and progress in games.

8 LEAVE A LIKE

Once you've played a game for a while and are used to what to do and how good it may be, you can 'leave a like' and tell the ROBLOX community if you think it's a good game. Just click on the thumb up icon from the home page (you may need to verify your email address, so make sure the adult who helped set up your account is there to assist). Of course if you didn't rate the game, click on the thumb down button!

WHAT DID YOU THINK OF {Game Name}?

358   153

9 CREATE A GAME

Don't just play the games – design and build them, too! That's what helps make ROBLOX so incredible, because the developers are fans, just like you.

ROBLOX Studio is the tool you need to build your own worlds and it is accessed through the Create tab. It may seem complicated at first, but thankfully there are step-by-step tutorials and instructions to follow, so that you can begin to use your imagination to the max. If you have done some sort of basic coding before, either at school or home, then ROBLOX Studio is for you.

Decide which genre of game you want to build and make sure that you use the templates on offer. This will save you lots of time as you explore and play with the options you have. You will likely make mistakes, but you'll learn lessons very quickly, too! The Developer Forums and Hubs are also good places to pick up building tips. Good luck.

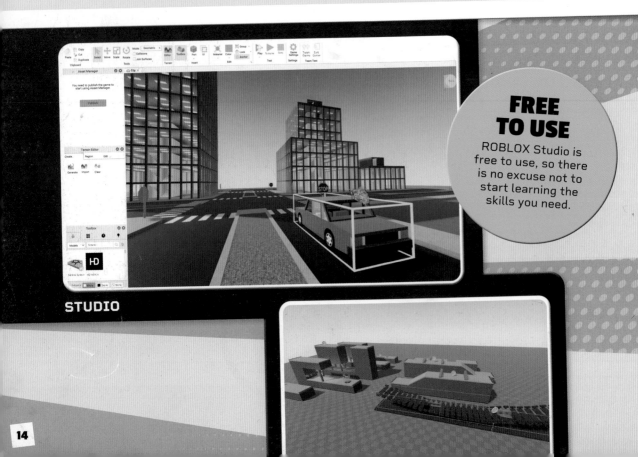

STUDIO

FREE TO USE

ROBLOX Studio is free to use, so there is no excuse not to start learning the skills you need.

10 PLAY WITH FRIENDS

ROBLOX can be a total friend fest! It's a safe and fun place for you and your mates to play games together and hang out.

As mentioned on page 6, text chatting and friend settings can be set up when you register for a ROBLOX account and be monitored by an adult. Access 'Friends' through the main homepage to see tabs including your followers, who you follow and any requests you have. You can also see if they are currently playing or if they are logged off, or 'Offline'. A good tip is to set up an alias for your friends, which means that you can identify them by their proper name and not their gaming tag. Only you will see the alias name, though. Use the chat typing function to speak with your friends. You can invite them to the game you're playing and maybe set a time for when you can all meet up again in the ROBLOX world!

Requests (290)

Friend 1 @friend1 Website	Friend 2 @friend2 Website	Friend 3 @friend3 Website
Ignore Accept	Ignore Accept	Ignore Accept
Friend 4 @friend4 Website	Friend 5 @friend5 Website	Friend 6 @friend6 Website
Ignore Accept	Ignore Accept	Ignore Accept
Friend 7 @friend7 Website	Friend 8 @friend8 Website	Friend 9 @friend9 Website
Ignore Accept	Ignore Accept	Ignore Accept
Friend 10 @friend10 Website	Friend 11 @friend11 Website	Friend 12 @friend12 Website
Ignore Accept	Ignore Accept	Ignore Accept

TOP TIP!
ROBLOX users on Xbox have the option to use the voice chat system.

Check out your requests and choose whether to accept them or not!

15

11 GET THE GEAR

Lots of games have gear – helpful items that give you abilities and options on screen.

There are around 10 main types and gear can range from weapons to power ups, explosives, vehicles and building tools. Not all types of gear are available in all games – it depends on the game developer's preference. Gear appears in your inventory bar so you can easily see the choices you have at your fingertips. Each one is assigned a hotkey so that you can quickly access it. Items can be rearranged through the backpack icon – it's best to keep the most important, or most used, gear in a prime slot. Take some time to keep your inventory and gear in good order and drag the items around, depending on what you'll need.

FAST FOOD OBBY

GAMES TO PLAY
- ISLAND ROYALE
- ULTIMATE DRIVING
- FAST FOOD OBBY

When you're against the clock and time is precious, that's when the ROBLOX pressure mounts up!

The universe can be a calming and peaceful place, but in some games the only target is to reach a level or complete a task before the time runs out – speed, skill and quick thinking are vital. If you're a fan of beating a countdown and can handle the heat as the seconds tick by, then read on! All types of game genres, from Battle Royale to Obstacle and Horror, can feature the looming tick-tocking of a clock winding down. The trick is to keep a level head and focus on the route to victory, while at the same time knowing that every move you make is precious.

ALONE: BATTLE ROYALE

CLIMB TIME
The Adventure game Climb Time was released in 2019 and is a cool obby-type platform set against the clock.

GAMES TO PLAY
- SPEED RUN 4
- ALONE: BATTLE ROYALE
- COUNTER BLOX

We know **ROBLOX** is fun because it means you're playing games and **NOT** stuck in the classroom. But a school-type adventure can still be an epic digital experience!

School games can come from Town & City, RPG and even Obstacle genres. Much of the gameplay is around attending school, developing your avatar, meeting friends and keeping yourself happy. In many games, if you're late to lessons, fail to follow instructions or don't navigate properly then you won't pick up rewards. It pays to be a perfect pupil! High School Life, which first opened for class back in 2012, had an update in 2021 which includes an incentive to keep playing and showing up at school. Visiting the butterfly near the spawn point reveals your time spent here – don't miss the chance to be a star student and get promoted to a higher rank!

HIGH SCHOOL LIFE

GAMES TO PLAY

- ROBLOXIAN HIGH SCHOOL
- ESCAPE SCHOOL OBBY
- HIGH SCHOOL LIFE

14 KEEP THE MUSIC ON

Whether you play on a console, PC, mobile or tablet, you can't underestimate the awesomeness of audio! Keeping sounds and music turned on, and played through your device or headphones, adds so much to the ROBLOX experience. Music will bring suspense to a murder mystery, comedy to a funny game and drama to a first person shooter. If you're facing an enemy, then you quite often hear them approaching or firing before you see them. 'Sounds' like a good plan, hey!

VEHICLE LEGENDS 02

TOP TIP!
To show you're a true music fan, why not add special headphones to your character from the Avatar Shop?

15 PLAY A BETA GAME

'BETA' means that a ROBLOX game is still in development, but there's enough built to reveal it to the community and let early play begin. So why load up a game that's not complete? Well, you get to see what work the developer has done so far, help to test parts of it and even give feedback on what's good and what's not. Plus, as an early player, you can often get a special badge. If you're creating your own game, playing other BETA games can give you tips and builder insight, too. The three game suggestions on the right were all in BETA stage in 2021.

STRUCID

GAMES TO PLAY
- STRUCID
- SOUTHWEST FLORIDA
- GRAPPLE SIMULATOR

19

16 WATCH THE BLOXYS

With awards such as Best New Game, Xbox Game of the Year, Video of the Year and Most Visits, the annual Bloxy awards is an event not to be missed. Accessed just like a regular game through the homepage, you can see the prizes handed out to the world's best and most exciting creators. With live music, special costumes to unlock and loads of exclusive content, turn up each year to see the best of the best!

FUN FACT!
Tower Defense Simulator, Brookhaven, Super Doomspire and Tank Warfare all won a Bloxy in 2021.

17 TIME TO TELEPORT

WORK AT A PIZZA PLACE

Bring a touch of magic to the screen! Teleporting can be very basic, such as choosing your spawn place on a map at the beginning of a game, or it can be a total game changer if you instantly teleport somewhere else during a vital moment. Teleporting is a tactic worth mastering and it can boost your scores or rewards in a flash. It's used in many ROBLOX universes, from Hide and Seek Extreme to Adopt Me! and Work at a Pizza Place.

ROBUX
In Work at a Pizza Place, you can pay Robux to teleport into the manager's position when it's available.

18 CHOOSE A COOL NAME

When you set up your avatar, think very carefully about the username you choose. You obviously want it to stand out, sound super cool and perhaps mean something to you as well. Try to be creative and invent a mega moniker for yourself – you could ask your ROBLOX friends what they think of it first. It would be a pain if you tagged yourself as something, only to regret it the next time you switched on!

AVATAR_NAME
@AVATAR_NAME

About

About

Tell the Roblox community about what you like to make, build, and explore...

AVATAR HOME

TOP TIP!
If you have already set your avatar name, it costs 1,000 Robux to change it again.

19 TAKE A TUTORIAL

Many ROBLOX games have the clever function of a quick in-game tutorial. Usually these are viewed and referred to for the first few times you play a game. Their purpose is to give you a speedy rundown of how to play and win – rules, tactics, controls, tips and so on. Even the best ROBLOX users will look at a tutorial, because it saves time learning a game from scratch.

BEE SWARM SIMULATOR

GAMES TO PLAY
- THEME PARK TYCOON 2
- BEE SWARM SIMULATOR
- BLOX HUNT

20 PLAY ON MOBILE

ROBLOX became available on smartphones in 2011. It gives gamers the chance to play while on the move or away from their usual home screen. There are limitations when using a smaller phone or tablet device, but being able to enter ROBLOXIA while relaxing in the garden or waiting for a bus is pretty cool.

TEXTING SIMULATOR

TOP TIP!
Smartphone fans can play the Texting Simulator game, launched by developer Kasius in 2018.

21 ESCAPE THE LAVA

THE FLOOR IS LAVA

Feeling the heat? Can't stand the flames? Take on a lava-tastic game and you'll really put your powers to the test! A classic in the survival range of games, lava-themed titles can come from Adventure, Horror, Obstacle and Comedy genres. The basic concept is to never touch the burning lava floor, which can bubble and rise beneath you – you often need to have good balance, jumping and coordination skills. Lava games can be good for just a quick adventure or keep you entertained for hours.

GAMES TO PLAY
- THE FLOOR IS LAVA
- CAN YOU SURVIVE LAVA?
- LAVA RUN

22 GET A DAILY BONUS

Did you know that lots of games dish out a daily bonus? This means you get rewards, tokens, items or coins just for logging in and playing each day. Easy stuff! Keep going back to the game to pick up these benefits. Plus the more time you spend playing and training, the better you'll become! Visit your favourite titles and you'll soon stack up a bunch of fun freebies that will give you an advantage.

GAMES TO PLAY

- ROCITIZENS
- NINJA LEGENDS
- SUPER EVOLUTION

SUPER EVOLUTION

23 COLLECT BADGES

You probably don't realise the number of badges you can collect in ROBLOX. Go to the Inventory tab from the Menu option and click Badges – here you will see all the awesome awards you've been given so far. Developers hand out badges for all sorts of things, from playing a game for the first time to reaching a level, defeating opponents, finding treasure and completing events. Wear each badge with pride!

FUN FACT!

FPS game Arsenal gives out a badge called Taco Tuesday, for taking out an enemy on that day!

If you want to get ahead in a game or stand out from the crowd, then scan through the Game Passes section in the Store tab.

A pass can offer you heaps of rewards and incentives such as levelling up, speed boosts, free respawns and double jump abilities. Passes can work across all types of games and really fast forward your progress. Getting a special nametag or avatar outfit makes other users aware of your VIP Game Pass status! Increasing the coins, jewels or money you can collect in a game is a common theme with passes. Being able to gobble up x4 or x5 the amount will make a huge difference to your cash stash. Some passes even give you Robux back. Sadly, game passes cost Robux, but if you have some spare, they can be a wise investment in games that you play all the time.

FASHION FAMOUS

TOP TIP!
Not all games will have a Game Pass section, so search your favourite titles to see what they offer.

GAMES TO PLAY
- ANIME FIGHTING
- TAPPING GODS
- CAR DEALERSHIP
- FASHION FAMOUS

JOIN PREMIUM

If you're super serious about ROBLOX and would like to get the very best from the game, you probably want to look at Premium.

It's a monthly subscription product that ranges from 450 to 1,000 and 2,200 levels, and it gives gamers loads of exciting extras to enhance their digital experience. Your account is credited with Robux each month, depending on how much you spend. This gives you access to Premium-only items and discounts in the Avatar Shop. Plus you can uncover exclusive boosts and levels during games, and have the Premium icon shown next to your name. If that's not impressive enough, Premium players also get 10 per cent more Robux whenever they buy the in-game currency. You can check out all the details by entering the Premium link from the main menu option.

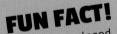

FUN FACT!
Premium replaced the original Builders Club membership subscription service offered by ROBLOX.

Roblox Premium

Get Premium

Robux every month
Receive Robux monthly on your subscription renewal date

Premium 450	Premium 1000	Premium 2200
450/mo	1000/mo	2200/mo
£4.59	£8.99	£18.49

TREASURE HUNT

All that glitters is gold... and silver, diamond and platinum!

Searching for treasure and shiny objects can lead to all sorts of ROBLOX adventures. Take on a treasure hunt mission and you could find yourself cast away on a ship, on a mysterious island, or even battling giant monsters. Always keep your eyes on the prize, though, and scoop the loot when you find or earn it! A treasure hunt can suit both new and experienced ROBLOX users. On a basic level, you are searching for gold and coins, and following map instructions. For more elite players, enemies must be conquered and complex tasks mastered before the rewards are finally placed in your pocket. Stealing treasure from those around is a common tactic, so be sure to watch out for sneaky thieves looking to cash in on your hard-earned discoveries.

TREASURE QUEST

TOP TIP!
In Treasure Quest you can view the inventory of another player to work out what's best to trade with them.

GAMES TO PLAY

- TREASURE QUEST
- BUILD A BOAT FOR TREASURE
- METAL DETECTOR SIMULATOR

27 PRIVATE SERVERS

Want to play a game privately with your friends or just the people you invite? Using a Private Server is the way to do it. Found on a game's main home page, just click on Servers to see if this function is offered. Some Private Servers are free to create but others may cost Robux to set up. Go for a free option, like in Adopt Me! or All Star Tower Defense, and you'll have an exclusive and exciting game just with your mates!

About

Private Servers

Price: ◆ 200

Visit this experience with friends and other people you invite.

Servers My Friends Are In

ROBLOX HOME

FUN FACT!

Many ROBLOX YouTube stars make their recordings on private servers so that they can make higher quality videos.

28 REV UP IN A RACE

The car racing and driving games in ROBLOX have millions of fans. Getting behind the wheel and spinning the tyres, while virtually sniffing the track dust, makes you feel like you're a real racer! From sports cars to super speed machines, rally tracks and even monster trucks, there's a vehicle and a game to suit your style. The quicker you are and the more success you have, the better the car you will get to control.

VEHICLE LEGENDS

GAMES TO PLAY
- **VEHICLE LEGENDS**
- **REDLINE DRIFTING**
- **DRIVING EMPIRE**

This sounds like a scary thing to do, especially as these types of games are usually in the Horror genre, but they can be great fun to play, too!

In Murder Mystery 2, which is by far the most visited game in this genre, the 12 players on the server are divided between 10 innocents, one sheriff and one dangerous killer. The killer's job is to take out as many innocents as possible without the sheriff identifying them. The room will work together to hunt down the evildoer – so that person must be very sneaky! The killer must be calm, clever and callous in their movements. In a murder mystery game, you never want to reveal your true identity and must take every opportunity to fool the crowd and blend in. When you're a good guy though, suspect everyone and keep your eyes peeled!

MURDER MYSTERY 2

TOP TIP!
Use the chat function to share information that can track down the murderer in the room.

GAMES TO PLAY
- MURDER MYSTERY 2
- MURDER PARTY
- IMPOSTOR

30 BOSS A TYCOON GAME

Tycoon games mean business – literally! Their purpose is to rake in money, rewards and benefits that build you up as a powerful player.

Some of them have the word tycoon in their game title, but others are less obvious. Work at a Pizza Place and My Store, for example, can be classed as Tycoon, even though they aren't placed in the genre. Tycoon games often involve building up a factory or a business. When you have grabbed your land, you'll need to earn and add new money-making equipment so that your cash flow begins to rise. Faster machines, more workers and increased customer visits all boost your bank balance. Don't forget to check out what your rivals are doing and learn tips to make your factory or company more profitable and powerful each day.

FUN FACT!
Retail Tycoon is based on the old Your Store Tycoon game, which was made by Dued1 – the brains behind Work at a Pizza Place!

RETAIL TYCOON

GAMES TO PLAY

- **RESTAURANT TYCOON 2**
- **RETAIL TYCOON**
- **SUPER HERO TYCOON**

As Fortnite became a huge videogame hit in 2018, more battle royale-style titles packed into the ROBLOX games page.

Classed in either Adventure, Fighting, FPS or All Genres sections, the basic idea is that you or your team are the last players standing after a weapons shootout. Usually based on a remote island, you choose a landing spot, scavenge for resources and guns and begin to plot the downfall of your enemies. With the clock ticking and space to operate shrinking, the pressure builds as your opponents reveal themselves. As well as needing an accurate shot and good knowledge of weapons, you must look after your health and replenish vital areas if you suffer damage. Teamwork is a must in a battle royale, so working as a unit and forcing others to make mistakes is a clever strategy. Be brave and smart to see off the rest.

TOP TIP!
Battle royale games usually have changes each season, so watch out for updated maps, weapons and items.

BATTLE ROYALE VIBE WAR

GAMES TO PLAY
- ISLAND ROYALE
- ALONE: BATTLE ROYALE
- BATTLE ROYALE VIBE WAR

SURVIVE A DISASTER

With billions of visits to a wide range of games, disaster survival platforms keep pulling in players year after year.

The reason that they remain so popular is because they are simple to understand, thrilling to play and need little expertise – though maybe a maybe a slice of luck! Up against the elements, your challenge may be to ride out an epic thunderstorm, dodge an earthquake or avoid a hurricane. Survive these devastating natural disasters and you'll live to see another mission. The king of this genre remains Natural Disaster Survival. With over 1.4 billion plays since 2008, this game is very addictive and drives you on to become an expert in predicting what the challenge will be and how to live through it. Tactics such as sheltering, building, looking for high ground and hiding in a safe structure are all options to explore.

SUPER BOMB SURVIVAL

TOP TIP!
Knowing what the incoming threat will be helps you to plan your escape. Try looking at the sky to see how the environment could change!

GAMES TO PLAY
- **NATURAL DISASTER SURVIVAL**
- **SUPER BOMB SURVIVAL**
- **SURVIVE THE DISASTERS 2**

Who doesn't want a cute companion to join them in the ROBLOX world!

Playing with and caring for pets can add so much to your gaming, giving you a creature to look after, feed and even help defend you at times. Pets can be a central part of a game, like in the fun Pet Show Dress Up, or play a smaller role in a simulator and RPG game. Pets are a cool part of MeepCity, where they are called 'Meeps', and owners can select their colour, name and style. Bolder and more adventurous games, including the smash hit Ninja Legends by Scriptbloxian Studios, can bring pets into play as well. These animals have a habit of popping up where you least expect them. They can help you earn rewards and train your skills, but more importantly they are also there for some furry fun and friendship!

Design your pet to the theme: Mini Me

01:45

Reindeer   Snow Owl   Ice Unicorn

PET SHOW DRESS UP

FUN FACT!
In Robloxian High School, you can ride and fly your precious pets as they get older.

GAMES TO PLAY
- PET SIMULATOR
- ROBLOXIAN HIGH SCHOOL
- PET SHOW DRESS UP
- MEEPCITY

LISTEN TO THE MUSIC

Over the years ROBLOX has become much more than just a digital game space.

One of the coolest developments is the arrival of virtual concerts. Music heroes record awesome content, like copies of their videos and stage performances, which is packaged into big musical events on the platform. At the end of 2020, US star Lil Nas X drew a crowd of 30 million as he featured his virtual concert. The songs Old Town Road, Panini and Rodeo went down a storm during the show! These concerts and pop star appearances are used in other areas, too. At the Bloxy awards in 2021, British band Royal Blood performed during the halftime show. Seeing all of these cool rock and pop star avatars playing and dancing on screen is crazy, but so entertaining. Look out for more exclusive concert performances!

This is an IRL performance by Royal Blood from 2017.

FUN FACT!
ROBLOX usually reveals behind-the-scenes videos of the artists recording their songs for these special concerts.

35 TOP THE BOARDS

The joy of being top of an in-game leaderboard is quite a rush! Whether it's an Obby game, Sports, Puzzles or FPS, sitting at the top of any ranking is a big boost to your confidence. Leaderboards come in a few styles – highest score, overall ability or all time hall of fame. Seeing your name among the game greats makes you stand out as a real ROBLOX hero!

GAMES TO PLAY
- MINER'S HAVEN
- CUBE DEFENSE

LEADERBOARD

36 SPEND ROBUX

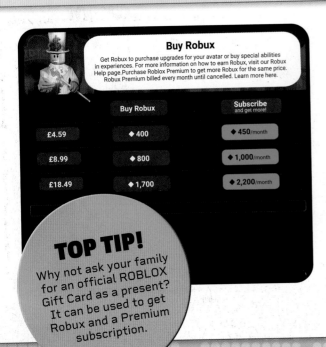

ROBLOX is totally free and does not need any form of real cash to download and play. That said, the in-game currency of Robux is available to use if someone you know is kind enough to buy some for you! Robux can add to the fun you have, letting you pick up extra cosmetics, upgrades and access to restricted zones. Don't worry if you don't have it in your pocket, but enjoy it if you're one of the lucky ones who does.

TOP TIP!
Why not ask your family for an official ROBLOX Gift Card as a present? It can be used to get Robux and a Premium subscription.

37 GET IN THE WATER

Don't be a land lover for all of your ROBLOX life – dip in your toes and dive into the wet stuff every now and then! Water-based games can see you swimming for survival or to reach an island, and travelling on a boat to finish your mission. Sharkbite is an epic game on the water! Even if your boat capsizes, you can still take refuge from the fearsome predators while sitting on top of your overturned vessel.

SHARKBITE

FUN FACT!
In the Hole in the Wall Comedy game, the objective is to actually keep out of the water!

38 GET CREATIVE

Did you know that game developers can also create funky accessories to dress up your avatar? Accessed through the shop and listed under Community Creations, there are all sorts of exclusive items, from hats and hairstyles to bags, sunglasses and masks. You can filter searches through bestsellers or by most recent and cost. You can even click on the creators to see what they are currently wearing and get a full rundown of all the items they have made.

Community Creations

Aesthetic low piggytails in
By @Archi_tecture
◆ 75

Black messy Boy Hair
By @Rush_X
◆ 75

Adorbs black long hair
By @Zeyacti
◆ 85

Popular Girl Blonde Hair
By @bunnexh
◆ 90

Snow Fuzzy Headpand
By @Ellzd
◆ 70

Black Fuzzy Headband
By @Ellzd
◆ 70

Black Messy Popular Boy Hair
By @Rush_X
◆ 75

Vintage Glasses
By @WhoToTrus
◆ 125

Fur Lyfe
By @GuestCapone
◆ 69

Lazy low buns
By @Beeism
◆ 90

TOP TIP!
Before you spend precious Robux on a Community Creation, click the 'try on' button to see how an item will look on your avatar.

39 MINE AND CRAFT

Minecraft is played a gazillion times a day by gamers all over the world!

On ROBLOX, you can get a Minecraft-style fix as well – thanks to a host of top sandbox titles such as MineWorld and Minerscave. These mix elements of building, trading, crafting, teamwork and taking on opponents. In MineWorld you can select helpful tools like the shield sword, meteor staff and lightning orb to aid your progression, while keeping stock of the elements you have for your important crafting.

Each server has its own map and your imagination can run away with you in this world. Building sim games offer a good Minecraft experience, too. Blocks, by Darin's Games, is simple in its design but offers a good creation experience as users get to grips with building blocky structures. With up to nine others on the server, you can trek over to another user's plot and spy on what they are building!

MINEWORLD

TOP TIP!
Build and Survive features waves of manic zombies and robots, so creating a destructive weapon is vital.

GAMES TO PLAY
- **BUILD AND SURVIVE**
- **MINING SIMULATOR**
- **MINEWORLD**

ROBLOX isn't all about beating zombies, catching escaped crims and racing around in speed machines.

There are plenty of opportunities to stop and tell some jokes and mess around. The Comedy genre has LOL-based games that will get you chuckling and smiling in front of other players or a crowd! You have to check out Comedy Club by EndlessAmazement. The pressure will be on as you take to the stage and either reveal your own joke or pick a random one provided for you. Watch out, though, as rotten tomatoes could be chucked your way if the joke goes down badly. When you're not on stage, relax and enjoy the other gags being told. With all the jokes being cracked, you should soon become a pro comedian in real life!

THE COMEDY ELEVATOR

FUN FACT!
ROBLOX likes to play April fools – on 1 April 2019 it claimed to have made a ROBLOX console that could stream to your refrigerator!

GAMES TO PLAY

- COMEDY CLUB
- THE COMEDY ELEVATOR

41 JOIN A GROUP

Do you want to hang out with other ROBLOX users who have similar passions and likes to you?

If you're nodding now, then check out the Groups function from the main homepage. Groups were first added back in 2009 and had a big update 10 years later. They let you join a space with others like you to share knowledge and tips for the games you enjoy. You can also see which groups your friends are in – there are lots of them listed under different categories. Try using the search bar to look for a group you would like.

Just type in a key word and you'll see something linked to it. You can click on a group for a brief description about it and to see members who are part of it, plus any Store or Affiliate links. One of the best things about Groups is the Wall. Here is the place to post fun messages for other users. They may be about a recent game update or development, or perhaps something linked to your favourite game's developer.

GROUP

TOP TIP!
A group may ask you to post about the 'QoTD'. This means Question of the Day!

CREATE A GROUP

When you know your way around the Group function, you'll soon want to create your own.

This gives you the chance to set up a place where gamers like you can chat and play together. It's really easy to set up by clicking on the 'Create Group' option on the Groups page. Spend some time thinking of a cool, easy-to-read and unique name for the group. It's also a good idea to scribble a brief description about the group, but this is not essential. You will need a striking emblem to give interested users an idea of what the group is about. This can be an image you have or one you create, so be imaginative! An important thing to consider with creating a group is whether anyone can join or if you want to manually approve the join requests. At first you may want the option to approve, just so that you can check who is being allowed in. Finally, you will need some Robux to create a group, which was priced at 100 Robux in 2021.

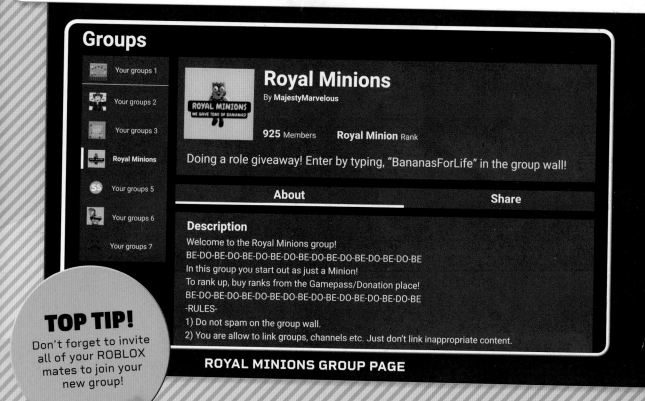

Groups

Your groups 1
Your groups 2
Your groups 3
Royal Minions
Your groups 5
Your groups 6
Your groups 7

Royal Minions
By MajestyMarvelous

925 Members   Royal Minion Rank

Doing a role giveaway! Enter by typing, "BananasForLife" in the group wall!

About   Share

Description
Welcome to the Royal Minions group!
BE-DO-BE-DO-BE-DO-BE-DO-BE-DO-BE-DO-BE-DO-BE-DO-BE
In this group you start out as just a Minion!
To rank up, buy ranks from the Gamepass/Donation place!
BE-DO-BE-DO-BE-DO-BE-DO-BE-DO-BE-DO-BE-DO-BE-DO-BE
-RULES-
1) Do not spam on the group wall.
2) You are allow to link groups, channels etc. Just don't link inappropriate content.

ROYAL MINIONS GROUP PAGE

TOP TIP!
Don't forget to invite all of your ROBLOX mates to join your new group!

43 LOBBY LEARNING

Don't dismiss the lobby area as just the starting point to rush away from and start the real action.

Nope – learning what to get from a lobby can give you a good head start each time you play! This space can offer you lots of choices, from which server or game to join to cosmetic options, customizations and settings. In the lobby there's no real-game pressure, so use it to understand the avatar controls and read any rules. You can usually see helpful leaderboards and rankings, too.

Some lobbies give you the chance to choose the next game (although this may need Robux), or a training area to help get you up to speed for the actual activity ahead of you. Developers do spend ages making the lobby a cool place to chill out in, so always look around them and check out what benefits you can get.

WORLD ZERO

FUN FACT!
There's even a Bloxy Award for Best Lobby, won by Rumble Quest and Epic Minigames in the past!

GAMES TO PLAY
- EPIC MINIGAMES
- SHINDO
- WORLD ZERO

44 WRITE ABOUT YOU

Don't worry – this won't be like extra schoolwork! In ROBLOX it helps to tell your friends and the wider community a little about yourself. This will help them get to know you, accept your friend request and play your games (if you have created any). ROBLOX gives you the space to reveal a little about your gaming likes, in the 'About' section in your main avatar page. Here, you have up to 1,000 letters to use, but keep it simple to start with. And never reveal any personal details!

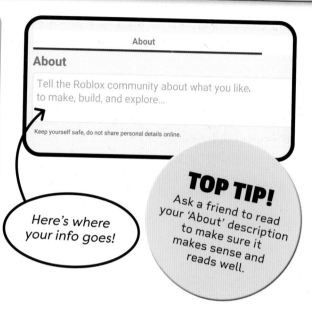

About

About

Tell the Roblox community about what you like. to make, build, and explore...

Keep yourself safe, do not share personal details online.

Here's where your info goes!

TOP TIP!
Ask a friend to read your 'About' description to make sure it makes sense and reads well.

45 DO SOME TRADING

When a player has the Trading option enabled on their account settings, it means that they can swap items with another player who also has it. So, if you like something that your friend has, you could swap it for something you have. Both users must agree on the trade. If you want to sweeten the deal and really tempt the exchange, there's the option to include some Robux, too!

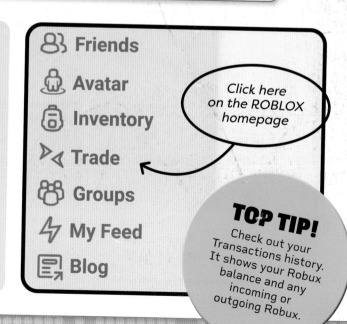

Friends

Avatar

Inventory

Trade

Groups

My Feed

Blog

Click here on the ROBLOX homepage

TOP TIP!
Check out your Transactions history. It shows your Robux balance and any incoming or outgoing Robux.

46 USE PROMPTS

This is a neat trick that you may not be using to the maximum.

On the ROBLOX homepage under your avatar name, there are three functions related to game playing: Continue Playing, Recommended For You and Friends Playing. Each of these offers a great way to explore the games that could be perfect for you, but without having to do loads of searching. Friends Playing reveals what some of your mates are currently enjoying. Have a flick through and try some. If you have forgotten a game that you played a while back, you can open Continue Playing to see the most recent ones that you have tried. Looking in here could remind you of an old fave you played ages ago. Finally, Recommended For You lists games that ROBLOX reckons you'll enjoy. Try some and see if they are right!

Continue

Spider

👍 73% 👤 9.9K

Brookhaven RP

👍 86% 👤 421.5K

Ride a rocket to the space station

👍 77% 👤 38

Space Combat Tycoon

👍 83% 👤 100

SPACE SAILOR

👍 90% 👤 544

Would You Rather..?

👍 88% 👤 518

Would You Rather 2?

👍 84% 👤 279

[4 MIL SALE!] QS Energy

👍 86% 👤 63

NEW!) Escape The Arcade

👍 42% 👤 63

TOP TIP!

Expand the 'see all' option for a more extensive breakdown of the games being shown.

47 WATCH TEASERS

When you're deciding which game to play from the hundreds on show, having a teaser video to watch is really handy. Go to the game's homepage and a video may be displayed at the top, alongside a few action images. The vid will be a brief but exciting. Look at what the game is all about. Watch it through to help you decide if you'd like to spend time actually playing it!

PILOT TRAINING FLIGHT SIMULATOR

FUN FACT!
Game videos must be under 30 seconds – ROBLOX is very strict about this!

GAMES TO PLAY
- SUPER HERO LIFE III
- PILOT TRAINING FLIGHT SIMULATOR
- VEHICLE LEGENDS

FUN FACT!
In Hide and Seek Extreme, glue drops and stun rays can help trap a player.

48 SET TRAPS

Whether it's an actual trap item or setting a trap to lure someone, traps are tops in ROBLOX! In the massively popular Piggy game, trap tools are used to stop a user from escaping. If you're a fan of the battle royale fighter games, a common tactic is to drop an item, then wait for a player to come along and give you the chance to easily eliminate them. Sneaky!

PIGGY

GAMES TO PLAY
- PIGGY
- HIDE AND SEEK EXTREME
- ALONE: BATTLE ROYALE

49 PLAY A SIMULATOR

Commonly called 'sims' by ROBLUX users, there's a game to suit just about everything you can think of! If you're a fan of racing, building, pets, sports, mining or fishing, then search for a sim that will keep you busy for hours. Like role-playing games (RPG), a sim offers a slice of real-life action but with some twists and turns. Sims can be relaxing and simple, or complex and competitive!

BOSS FIGHTING SIMULATOR

FUN FACT!
If your parents always hassle you about keeping your bedroom tidy, then Cleaning Simulator could give you some tips!

GAMES TO PLAY
- DESTRUCTION SIMULATOR
- BOSS FIGHTING SIMULATOR
- GAS STATION SIMULATOR

50 PLAY SEASONAL GAMES

TOP TIP!
Virtual Block Studio, the people who make the wintery Snow Shoveling Simulator, offer 300 Robux to new users who join their Group.

SAVING CHRISTMAS

Whether you want to get in the festive Christmas spirit, your school summer holidays are coming, OR it's time to hunt for Easter eggs, ROBLOX always delivers a big helping of super seasonal fun. Whatever the time of year and no matter what big events are coming up, just look for a themed game and you'll get right into the celebrations. Whether it's snowing or sunny outside, there's no time to waste!

GAMES TO PLAY
- SAVING CHRISTMAS
- EASTER OBBY
- SUMMER CAMP HANGOUT

51 VISIT PARTY PLACE

The clever folk who run ROBLOX always come up with fresh and fun ideas – Party Place is exactly one of those! Using a venue from the cool Bloxy awards, it's a flashy arena where you and your mates can chill out together and chat. The party host can control the music, and there's loads of space to roam and quests to complete, plus you can ride an inflatable unicorn on water. What's not to like?

PARTY PLACE

TOP TIP!
Party Place is a wacky venue full of crazy neon signs and symbols, so you may need sunglasses!

52 MAKE THINGS TOUGH

Life is full of challenges and tough decisions, and that should also be the case in ROBLOX! You could cruise through games and activities in basic mode, but the real heroes crank up the pressure. If you're in the puzzle game Escape Room, you definitely don't settle for the easy option. You're already playing one of the toughest games out there!

FUN FACT!
Escape Room actually won the Bloxy for Hardest Game!

ESCAPE ROOM

Maths, nature, history... these can all be learnt about in ROBLOX, but of course it will be in a fun way, too!

There isn't a specific genre called 'education' or 'facts', so this kind of game can be tricky to find, but type in the right search key word and you will see plenty of choices. The Math Obby is a test for your brain and your fingertips, and try Untamed Planet to boost your knowledge of animals and environments. With some of these games, clues and codes are given out or need to be cracked as you move around. It's good practice to have a pencil ready to scribble things down, to help you input them later on. If you play with a friend, teamwork is useful for working out tough answers – two brains are always better than one!

UNTAMED PLANET

TOP TIP!
In Untamed Planet, Premium subscribers get one extra WildCoin every minute they play.

GAMES TO PLAY
- UNTAMED PLANET
- THE MATH OBBY
- TEAMWORK PUZZLES
- MATH SIMULATOR

Some virtual reality (VR) headsets are compatible with ROBLOX.

Link up to this if you have the tech and you'll take your gaming to another level! VR has the ability to immerse a gamer in the digital world and give them the feeling of being in total control. By placing the headset on, you can see the world change in front of you. You will need to search for the games that have strong VR enhancement. VR games are also playable in a non-VR mode, so you can still enjoy them with friends who don't have a headset. So what is playing with VR really like? Try out the VR Hands game, created by Mad-Viking Production in 2020, as your first experience. You'll get to grips (quite literally!) with VR up close and understand the feeling of having it at your fingertips.

LASER TAG VR

TOP TIP!

Look for games with the 'VR' symbol next to their name, or placed in the main image box on the Games homepage.

GAMES TO PLAY

- COOK BURGERS
- LASER TAG VR
- KOALA CAFÉ
- RAGDOLL SIM

55 CELEBRATE

Keep 1 September as a big date in your diary. Every year on this day, ROBLOX reveals something extra cool to help them celebrate their birthday!

Launched in 2006, the game always marks this big occasion in some way. In 2020 they gave away a free code to pick up a flash 14th birthday cape for your avatar. Gamers sporting this always make plenty of players jealous! Other awesome exclusives on the ROBLOX birthday have included special cakes, birthday cake masks, sunglasses, hats and wing-themed backpacks. A badge has also been made available to mark the event. If your own birthday also happens to be on 1 September, then it's a double celebration and time for a party... cakes, funny hats, presents and dancing all round please!

TOP TIP!
Birthday items are usually available for 10 days to two weeks after being released on 1 September.

Try On | 3D

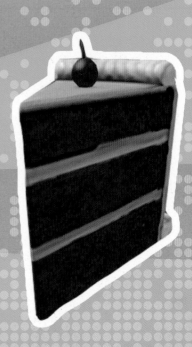

Sometimes you want to record the games you play and the achievements you make.

Luckily ROBLOX has a neat function that let's you do that very easily. If you use this feature, you can watch your own gaming videos over and over again! When you're in a game, just go to the menu button and click the Record tab. Pressing this option means your on screen adventure will be saved, ready to be watched later through the 'my videos' link. This is exactly how all your favourite

YouTubers record their content as well. If you record lots of stuff, you might want to think about adding some audio commentary and then sharing the clips with your friends, if you have permission to do this. Not every game you play is worth recording, but if you have a new update to explore or some cool items and gear to show off, then hit that button!

This is the record tab.

This is what it looks like when you are recording.

TOP TIP!
You can also take an in-game screenshot of yourself playing your favourite missions and adventures.

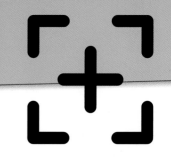

Did you know that you can change the camera settings of a game?

As long as the game is not locked to a certain setting, you have the option of switching from the default, which is usually Classic, to Follow. This changes your perspective from being able to see your avatar on screen to one where you become invisible, apart from any equipped tools or weapons. It's totally your choice which of these you prefer. The Classic view is perhaps easier to use, especially if you're a new player, plus you get to see what your avatar is wearing and the moves it makes. Follow puts you 'in the moment' and is probably more exciting and intense – you get to see through the eyes of your character. Switches can be made during a game if needed. Play around to see which you prefer!

Classic view

Follow view

58 HAVE FUN FARMING

Even if you have never set foot on a farm before and have zero interest in tractors, crops and animals, you should still give a farm game a go. Get muddy and you'll soon be smiling! You'll have the chance to sit behind the wheel of huge machinery, work with your fellow farmers, expand and build your field and look after the hungry animals. Unlocking more equipment can speed up your farming, giving you more to trade and cash in.

FUN FACT!
In the My Farm game, golden chickens lay golden eggs – look out for this prized poultry!

GAMES TO PLAY
- **FARMING AND FRIENDS**
- **MY FARM**
- **FARM LIFE**
- **MILLIONAIRE FARM TYCOON**

59 FOLLOW A GAME

This is so simple, but a very rewarding tip for new or elite ROBLOX users! For the games that you really enjoy, you can click the 'follow' button and keep totally up to date with any changes, news, codes and updates made to it. It's easy to spot on a game's homepage – it is found underneath the green play arrow. Now you'll never miss a major development again!

Miner's Haven
By berezaa Games™

Click here on a game's homepage to follow the game.

Favorite   Follow   450K+   96k+

GAMES TO PLAY
- **SUPER GOLF**
- **MARBLE MANIA**
- **EMERGENCY RESPONSE: LIBERTY COUNTY**

60 GET 'AMONG' IT

When the video and mobile game Among Us exploded in popularity in 2020, similar games soon rocked up on the ROBLOX games page.

It sparked a mega surge for similar murder mystery-type action, with crewmates searching for the evil players and working together to share clues and information. If you haven't enjoyed an experience like this yet, then get undercover and get involved! These games often need some practice, but they are pretty easy to pick up.

Becoming familiar with each map and knowing routes, including options for escape routes, is important. You will need to stay alert to what you see around you, and if you are chosen as the impostor, you'll have to act super sneaky! Use all the tools that you can, including CCTV cameras, door passes and codes.

AMONG US ZOMBIES

TOP TIP!
Code! Amongst Us, by Wizard Studios, clocked up over 225 million visits within eight months of being released.

GAMES TO PLAY
- CREWMATES
- CODE! AMONGST US
- AMONG US ZOMBIES

Come on, don't be shy! We all love doing cool and silly things up on stage in a talent show, whether it's at school or at home for fun.

ROBLOX has games based around the popular talent show concept. The tasks you need to complete can call on a range of talents, from simple obstacle courses through to parkour activities, singing and dancing. Players earn reputation, or rep, for successful performances. They can then use their rep to become the show's host or a judge.

Being part of the audience or audition roles does not cost any rep. Rep is picked up by being successful in talent performances – don't forget to rehearse your moves and skills in the free training areas. Above all else, don't get stage fright and crumble on the spot!

ROBLOX'S GOT TALENT

TOP TIP!
Get the Unlimited Host badge in ROBLOX Talent Show and you can be the host without using up your rep.

GAMES TO PLAY
- ROBLOX TALENT SHOW
- ROBLOX'S GOT TALENT

Well, yeah – of course you want to run and escape from the clutches of a zombie!

Being caught and held by one of these ghastly green ghouls is not nice at all. That shouldn't mean you avoid playing any of the ROBLOX zombie games, though, because facing up to and tackling these horrid creatures is a laugh, too. Zombies tend to be slow and are often unarmed, so with the right tactics and weapons in hand you can outsmart them. In Zombie

Attack, the main green baddie to look out for is the Boss Zombie. Target and destroy him and the waves of smaller zombies around you will feel like no threat at all. Apocalypse Rising also requires you to smash through these monsters, and in Zombie Rush, why not switch sides and see what it's like to become one? Good luck.

ZOMBIE ATTACK

FUN FACT!
You can use flying machines to attack the cruel creatures in Zombie Defense Tycoon!

GAMES TO PLAY

- ZOMBIE ATTACK
- ZOMBIE UPRISING
- ZOMBIE APOCALYPSE

63 GET SPOOKY

Playing against zombies should always remind you of Halloween – and to have fun at this time of the year.

Actually, Halloween is so popular with ROBLOX gamers that you can experience it all-year round! You can get a ghostly dose of Halloween in lots of different ways, like dressing up in spooky gear or visiting a haunted castle. The Horror genre is where most Halloween games are found, but they also appear in Action and RPG. Halloween, by ChainLemonadeStudios, is a small game that has grown in popularity recently (since around October and November). The makers even tell you to "turn up the volume for the best experience". This means that a lot of the fearsome tasks you face are boosted by the scary sounds connected to them. Look and listen for danger at every turn!

TOP TIP!
Search for 'Ghost' in the Games area to reveal more frightening adventures to explore.

HALLOWEEN NIGHT

GAMES TO PLAY

- HALLOWEEN NIGHT
- TRICK OR TREAT
- NIGHTMARES

64 VISIT THEME PARKS

Found in genres like Building, Adventure and Town & City, theme park games pop up all the time.

If you enjoy thrills and spills, highs and lows and dazzling displays, join in and see what the fuss is all about. Even if you're scared of things like roller coasters and heights, you can always design your own park and then just sit back and count the cash earned from visitors! Theme Park Tycoon 2 leads the way with popularity, and is all about building an attraction which others will love enough to keep coming back to. Theme Park Universal Studios Roblox is a well-made alternative. It brings in movie-themed rides from blockbusters such as *Jurassic Park*, *The Incredible Hulk* and *Harry Potter*. Hold on tight for a journey full of surprises.

THEME PARK TYCOON 2

FUN FACT!
Mix attractions with ghosts and zombies by playing Escape The Theme Park Obby.

GAMES TO PLAY
- THEME PARK TYCOON 2
- THEME PARK UNIVERSAL STUDIOS ROBLOX

You will no doubt know of Hide and Seek Extreme, which has had over 1.5 billion visits since it began in 2015.

It's a smash hit seeking game that's simple enough to understand straight away, but with enough quirks and twists to keep people playing for hours. That's the beauty of any hiding game – they are easy but very, very addictive! For an interesting take on this style of game, have a go on Among Us: Hide and Seek. It's different to the usual Among Us-type murder events because the innocent players know who the impostor is and must run away at the start to evade capture. Mega Hide and Seek is another to try. When a round is in progress and you're watching, toggle between players to spy on where they are lurking!

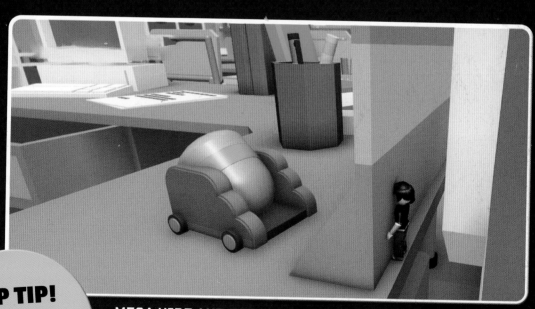

MEGA HIDE AND SEEK

TOP TIP!
If you have bright clothing, huge hats and a backpack, you'll be easier to spot when you're hiding!

GAMES TO PLAY
- **HIDE AND SEEK EXTREME**
- **AMONG US: HIDE AND SEEK**
- **MEGA HIDE AND SEEK**

66 CRACK THE PUZZLE

It's time to think smartly and solve puzzles, riddles and problems! ROBLOX can test your skills in lots of ways. Whether playing solo or as a team, overcoming a challenge is always a big achievement. These games have a different adrenaline buzz to action and adventure titles, but getting answers correct and plotting your path is very rewarding. You can even take a quiz to test how well you know ROBLOX!

THE ROBLOX QUIZ

GAMES TO PLAY
- PUZZLE ROOMS
- THE ROBLOX QUIZ
- PUZZLE BOX

67 TRY AN ORIGINAL GAME

FUN FACT!
The very first ROBLOX game, made in 2006, was called Rocket Arena. It's not playable any more, though!

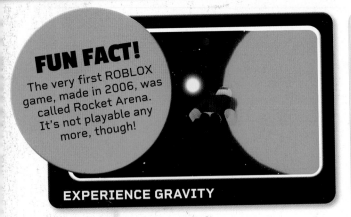

EXPERIENCE GRAVITY

To get the full ROBLOX gaming experience, take yourself back to a time before tablets, smartphones and even MeepCity ruled the world. In this different era, games like Base Wars and Experience Gravity were the places where users hung out and battled each other. Try playing them for yourself now. They won't be as slick or exciting as newer titles, but jump in and appreciate what the ROBLOX universe was like back in the day!

GAMES TO PLAY
- BASE WARS
- CLASSIC: CROSSROADS
- EXPERIENCE GRAVITY

68 PLAY THE NAME GAME

Stuck for a game to play and don't know what to look for? Play the name game then! Just type your name into the search bar and see what the options are – you could find something cool and crazy! If your first name doesn't produce any results, try your surname, your best friend's, or your pet's... There will be choices to make and new challenges to accept. A name is the aim of the game!

FUN FACT!
The Builderman ROBLOX character is the game's founder, David Baszucki. He has 69 million followers in the game!

69 READ CLUES

This seems like a simple instruction, but looking for clues and helpful signs during games will get you much further. Ninja Legends, for example, has important instructions and pointers planted around, so don't forget to slow down and follow them. Even basic guidance could boost you to a previously locked area and increase the coins and items you collect. Always read any clues that you find!

NINJA LEGENDS

GAMES TO PLAY
- NINJA LEGENDS
- SUPER POWER FIGHTING SIMULATOR

GET SPORTY

From football to basketball, tennis to running, and boxing to motor racing, there's a sports game to get you active!

Whether you're a natural sports fan or more of an armchair supporter, search through the hundreds of titles to discover one that suits you. Popular football (soccer) games, TPS: Ultimate Soccer and TPS: Street Soccer are both made by TAYFUN 7 and give a good pitch experience. Kick Off is very simple good team fun for multiple players.

Weight Lifting Simulator sees you set targets to boost your strength and train to become a powerful performer. If it's speed that you're looking for, then Speed Run Simulator is packed with pacey obstacles and adventures, though it is less of a traditional sports game.

KICK OFF

FUN FACT!
In Gymnastics Gymnasium, you can buy a selfie stick so you can take cool snaps with your friends.

GAMES TO PLAY

- KICK OFF
- WEIGHT LIFTING SIMULATOR
- FOOTBALL FUSION

71 FIVE-MINUTE FRENZY

Get the stopwatch ready! If you want to try a stack of new games quickly and pick one to stick with, choose five you've never played before, then play each one for just five minutes. In the frantic 300 seconds you'll spend on each, you must decide which to go with and get better at. Perhaps you'll quickly know the one to choose at once, or you may just need a gut reaction to select. Ready, set, go!

72 BE A BATTLE BUILDER

This is another ROBLOX challenge against the clock. You and a friend, or group of friends, can join a building game, then see who can create the coolest structure in a set time. You'll need to be speedy with the tools, but also creative in your designs so that you impress the others. Build Battle is the perfect training ground for this – don't worry if you're a beginner – you'll soon improve.

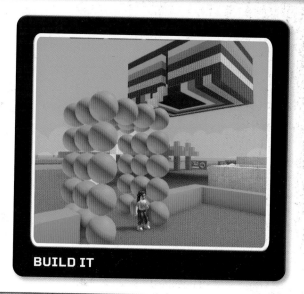

BUILD IT

GAMES TO PLAY
- **BUILD BATTLE**
- **BUILDING ARCHITECT**
- **BUILD IT**

73 BE A BADDIE

The good guys don't have all the fun! Every now and then, try switching on your evil side and playing a ROBLOX game as a baddie.

You may have to steal items, evade capture, escape from a fortress and generally cause havoc. It can be a welcome relief from doing what's right all the time – and it's lots of fun going up against the good characters! Many games have the option to choose which side to play for. Jail games, like Prison Life and Redwood Prison, allow you to select which route you'll take.

It's great experience to play a variety of roles – both good and bad – to boost your skills and tactics. The popular Hunted game, by ColdDeveloper, sees the evildoer chase down nine others who have no weapons to defend themselves. But, after three minutes, the innocents suddenly get firearms and the tables turn on the baddie.

HUNTED

FUN FACT!
In Blox Fruits, players are either on the good Marines team, the bad Pirates team or in the middle with the Neutrals!

GAMES TO PLAY

- REDWOOD PRISON
- MURDER PARTY
- HUNTED

74 TAKE A VOTE

Voting, choosing, selecting, picking... it's basically the same thing in ROBLOX and is a common feature of many games.

It can be central to the gameplay, like choosing the best user creation in the cool building title Design It!, or just help you select which map to use, as with Phantom Forces and Flee the Facility. Don't get left behind and make sure your voice and opinion count! The Among Us-themed games (see page 52) are a total vote fest, with players having to decide which people to put forward as the potential murderers. For another helping of voting fun, try testing out, er, Outlaster! It's the successor to the brilliant Survivor game and is packed with choices to make. Losing teams must vote for a player to ditch after each round and Team Leaders must also be chosen. If you're a VIP, your vote counts double.

OUTLASTER

FUN FACT!
Remember, you can vote in the Bloxy awards each year!

GAMES TO PLAY
- OUTLASTER
- DESIGN IT!
- FLEE THE FACILITY

75 BREAKING RECORDS

Join the crowds and play the ROBLOX games that smash records, attract huge fan bases and set new trends!

While it's awesome to search out unique and small titles, playing the big ones shouldn't be missed. By summer 2021, Adopt Me! was the biggest game of all time, with over 22 billion visits – it enjoyed a record figure of 1.92 million gamers playing at the same time. Royale High, Jailbreak, MeepCity and Vehicle Simulator have all set new markers in recent years and picked up Bloxy awards. The Data Awards section of the Bloxys show the number-bashing titles over the previous 12 months. With awards given for areas like Most Returning, Highest Rated, Highest Average Playtime and Most Improved, it's a strong indicator of great games that are hits across PC, console and mobile.

FUN FACT!
Piggy clocked up a staggering 1 billion visits in just 83 days after release!

VEHICLE SIMULATOR

GAMES TO PLAY
- WELCOME TO BLOXBURG
- ROYALE HIGH
- VEHICLE SIMULATOR

JUMP INTO AN OBBY

Obstacle course games have been one of the most popular genres for years and years!

The 'obby' titles keep getting tens of millions of visits, whether it's to tried and tested ones or new obstacle courses that pop up on the Games page. An obby delivers quick games, exciting action, a variety of challenges and inspires a thirst to keep improving and reaching new levels. It can seem like you'll never reach the end, and in some cases you won't! If you have never tried a straight obby game before, chances are you have done an obby in other games. Floor is Lava, Baldi Basics and Escape the Butcher will get you running and jumping to continue your quests. You need quick fingers and steady controls to master an obstacle adventure, so make sure that you are comfortable with all the functions at your fingertips. Reaching checkpoints is very helpful and stops you restarting further back.

ESCAPE YOUTUBE OBBY

TOP TIP!
Don't just search for obby games in the Obstacle genre. Look in Adventure, Simulator and Survival, too.

GAMES TO PLAY
- COOL PARKOUR OBBY
- MEGA EASY OBBY
- ESCAPE YOUTUBE OBBY

77 WAIT A WHILE

You may have the fastest machine and WiFi in the world, but your favourite games could still take a little while to load on screen. So be patient, sit tight and get ready for when the action unfolds! Even a game like Ninja Legends needs you to wait while duels are settled and the timer counts down. Natural Disaster Survival can leave you hanging for ages... but hang on in there!

TOP TIP!
Use any waiting time to check out new game features, leaderboards and item updates.

NATURAL DISASTER SURVIVAL

GAMES TO PLAY
- NINJA LEGENDS
- NATURAL DISASTER SURVIVAL

78 ROCK IN R6

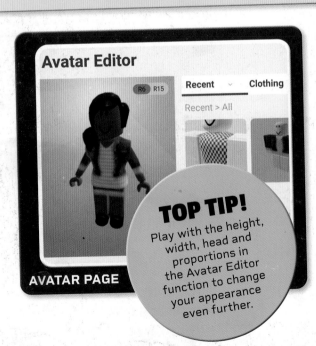

Avatar Editor

R6 R15

Recent ⌄   Clothing

Recent > All

AVATAR PAGE

TOP TIP!
Play with the height, width, head and proportions in the Avatar Editor function to change your appearance even further.

These days avatars usually take the shape of R15, which uses a sophisticated look to make your character's movements very smooth on screen. Before this was made available in 2016, users had to set up their look with the R6 system that had just six major body parts. It appears very blocky and basic, but it can give you an original ROBLOX vibe and make you stand out from other gamers around you. Go to the Avatar Editor function to experiment.

79 TRY GAME KITS

The ROBLOX Studio area is where you create games for others to play. Here, game kits are often made available. These have all the basics you should need to get a certain game type set up and running. Think of it like a template shortcut. Recently, ROBLOX Battle Royale became popular as a tool to establish an island, install weapons and get fighters competing for victory. It's an awesome time saver.

80 FOLLOW HACK WEEK

Every year since 2014, all ROBLOX employees take part in an event called Hack Week. What the occasion produces is a bunch of new ideas that will improve ROBLOX in the future. All the workers can make suggestions, big or small, to make our gaming better. Recently, location-based mobile games, heatmaps, live ops support, automated chat emotions and sound absorption techniques have been raised. Sounds geeky, but soon these factors could become real in ROBLOX!

TOP TIP!
ROBLOX puts Hack Week video highlights on its blog page and YouTube channel.

81 CASH IN ON DEV EX

If you're keen enough to create ROBLOX games and make them popular, you will no doubt become interested in the Developer Exchange Program. Nicknamed DevEx by the community, this is the system that lets creators earn real money from games that others like playing. You must be registered through Premium and have at least 100,000 earned Robux in your account so that you can start cashing in.

82 PAY TO PLAY

MIGHTY OMEGA

Most games cost nothing to join, but if you do have Robux, why not spend some and pay to play a game that really interests you? Sure, it's a pain handing over your precious currency, but it could be a wise investment if you unearth a new adventure that you play for ages. Check out all the reviews, comments, store options and server choices before clicking on the button to fork out the cash!

GAMES TO PLAY
- MIGHTY OMEGA
- TREELANDS
- BLOXTUBE

83 GET CODING

TOP TIP!
Premium users in Free Admin can take advantage of the Lucky Block option.

If you have used Scratch, or another basic coding tool at school or home, then why not try out a coding-based ROBLOX game. You don't need to be a computer genius or a top tech wizard to work them out – instructions and tutorials are included, plus in-game chats mean you can ask others for help. With over half a billion visits in under 18 months, Free Admin by Creator_Studio is a good starter game.

CODER SIMULATOR 2

GAMES TO PLAY
- FREE ADMIN
- CODER SIMULATOR 2

84 FIND UNIQUE GAMES

Look for that gem of a game that's totally different, a bit bonkers but still loads of fun! It can take a while to find one you like, so be prepared to search the Games page and do your research. Don't worry if it has low visitor numbers, because these games can be pretty tucked away and are not promoted much by ROBLOX.
Try Disguise Hunt for a blast of wacky hide and seek adventures!

DISGUISE HUNT

GAMES TO PLAY
- DISGUISE HUNT
- INFECTIOUS SMILE
- PINEWOOD COMPUTER CORE

85 EXPLORE ARCADES

Just because you're playing ROBLOX on a console, PC or mobile device, it doesn't mean you have to miss the thrill of an arcade game!

Classic machines where you can pick a prize, spin wheels and test your accuracy are all featured in a stack of super titles. If you love visiting an arcade and putting coins or tokens in to get a quick game going, then have a slice of this action. Arcade Island 2 has over 40 machines to choose from. These include prize catcher, target challenge, color wheel and balloon break extreme. You need chips to play (check your chip count in the dropdown list), and tickets can be won if you're successful. Purchasing chip rains and Game Passes will get you further, and most games rely on you having quick reflexes, tactical thinking... and a big slice of luck! Of course, if playing gets too much, you could always cook and serve meals in the restaurant instead.

ESCAPE THE ARCADE

TOP TIP!
Arcade Island 2 has a special machine game promotion where games are half price on Thursdays.

GAMES TO PLAY
- ARCADE ISLAND 2
- ARCADE EMPIRE
- ARCADE TYCOON
- ESCAPE THE ARCADE

Show off your slick winning moves by unleashing a cool dance routine!

ROBLOX's avatar dance function is called emotes. You can clap, jump, wave, point, breakdance, shuffle, act like a robot... and make hundreds more mega moves at the touch of a button! Lots of emotes are free and given away by ROBLOX during events and promotions. If you have Robux in your account, then stacking up on fancy emotes won't be a problem either. Emotes can be activated through the in-game chat function or the Emote Menu, which was created in 2019. A maximum of eight of your favourites can be equipped and selected in a split second. So when should you reveal your best moves? It's not a good idea to start strutting when you're under fire or leaping across obstacles, but if you have finished a level, set a high score or won a challenge, why not show off with an epic emote? Do your stuff and dance like a disco dude!

BROOKHAVEN

TOP TIP!

Themed animation packages can also be picked up, using Robux, through the Avatar Shop.

That's right – ask your teachers if you can explore ROBLOX at school and show them how educational and helpful it can be.

They may react by saying that gaming is not allowed in the classroom, but that's your chance to prove how cool and exciting the platform is – especially the Studio tools. Imagining and then building your own games, while learning techniques and tips to master the process is all made possible by clicking on the magical Create button. You may be able to start an afterschool or lunchtime ROBLOX club where other gamers like you can share ideas and successes! STEM (Science, Technology, Engineering, Maths) is being given a lot of focus at school right now and it's also at the core of what ROBLOX is all about. The people who work at the company, and the army of creators around the world, all started their passion for programming and gaming at school and home. Now it's down to you to show teachers how awesome ROBLOX is!

FUN FACT!
ROBLOX can encourage users to improve their skills at school and even has a special ROBLOX Education Team working for it.

88 USE BUNDLES

Bundles are a clever way to pick up a group of similar items in the Avatar Shop. Featured bundles will consist of a complete outfit, perhaps ranging from a superhero to a monster or sportsman avatar – and with a simple click the whole look is added to your Avatar Editor section. There are also clothing and body part bundles, so you can select a style that suits you, or maybe something completely different to make you stand out in a game lobby. Pick up a bundle and have a bundle of joy!

Avatar Shop

Category	Featured
Recommended	
View All Items	
Featured	
All Featured Items	
Featured Accessories	
Featured Aniamtions	
Featured Faces	
Featured Gear	
Featured Bundles	**Korblox**
Featured Emotes	**Deathspeaker**
Community Creations +	◆ 17,000
Premium +	
Collectibles +	
Clothing +	
Body Parts +	

TOP TIP!
Follow the official ROBLOX Group to see the bundles and items they frequently release.

89 ENTER COMPETITIONS

Unlike games such as Fortnite, FIFA and Rocket League, ROBLOX does not have official eSports competitions where regular gamers go head to head. But, there are chances to enter other cool contests to showcase your skills on the platform! The Winter 2021 Avatar Design Contest challenged users to come up with a unique character look based on one of a few themes, with the winner judged on creativity, realism and originality.

FUN FACT!
The Winter 2021 Avatar Design Contest winner scooped $500 in prize money and had their outfit appear in the Avatar Shop.

CHEAT PLAYING GAMES

Hang on – before you report us to the ROBLOX police, we mean 'cheating' in a legal way!

In many of the greatest games there are authorized ways to earn a smoother and quicker path to victory. You just need to know the route to take and it can be a proper game changer and time saver. Game passes (see page 24) that give you extra powers, lives, weapons and coins are an obvious cheat, but don't miss other chances to get ahead. In driving simulator games and some RPGs, like Brookhaven, unlocking a speed restriction gets you off to a flying start. In Escape the Carnival of Terror, teleporting and jet pack tools are another mega method of beating the opposition. In Find The Button, the 'skip room' paid-for cheat means you can avoid the locations you want to and look for passes that let you skip waiting times in other games.

BROOKHAVEN

GAMES TO PLAY
- BROOKHAVEN
- ESCAPE THE CARNIVAL OF TERROR
- FIND THE BUTTON

91 FLY IN THE SKY

There are all sorts of wonderful ways to take to the air in ROBLOX! Whether using your jetpack in a superhero game or cruising in a flight simulator, getting up in the clouds is really cool and exciting. Leave the losers behind on the ground and climb high! Pilot Training Flight Simulator and Plane Crazy give you a great taste of being in control of machines in the sky (it's tougher than you think!). Join Super Hero Life II for an awesome experience as a flying caped crusader.

TOP TIP!
In Super Hero Life II, closely monitor your health and energy bars as you fly.

GAMES TO PLAY
- PILOT TRAINING FLIGHT SIMULATOR
- PLANE CRAZY
- SUPER HERO LIFE II

92 WATCH RB BATTLES

Ever heard of the RB Battles Championship? It's an official campaign where 16 of the world's best ROBLOX YouTubers go head-to-head on a series of popular games. Their quest is to be crowned the ultimate player at the end of this tough test! You have the chance to vote for who you think will win, and earn exclusive rewards like Shield of Wisdom, RB Battle Packs and badges. The clashes are always fierce and the action red hot, so don't miss this annual four-week face-off.

FUN FACT!
The winner of the RB Battles Championship picks up a mighty one million Robux!

93 GET GEEKY

ROBLOX is great for getting your geek on, meaning it's a cool place for gamers who love all things techy, computer-based, science-y and a little bit nerdy. It revels in letting people explore fascinating subjects and areas. Quantum Science Energy Research Facility seems very intense when you first load it, but your geeky nuclear missions soon become clear and the race is on to save the day.

TOP TIP!
Quantum Science Energy Research Facility is full of lots of handy 'did you know' facts.

GAMES TO PLAY
- QUANTUM SCIENCE ENERGY RESEARCH FACILITY
- RO-BIO IMPROVED 2

94 BE BRAVE

SPIDER

FUN FACT!
Spider, by RoyStanford, reached over 500 million visits in less than a year!

Time to face your fears, gamers! In ROBLOX, you can be the bravest person in the world by tackling high-speed adventures, taking on scary monsters and facing up to extreme hazards. No-one would fancy a fight against an evil enemy in the real world, but in ROBLOXIA there are no limits. Even small things that might spook you at home, like spiders or cleaning your room, can be conquered!

GAMES TO PLAY
- SPIDER
- SHARK ATTACK
- GHOST SIMULATOR

95 HAVE A SNOW DAY

Everyone enjoys a snow day! The wintery weather sets in unexpectedly, you get the sled out and perhaps have to take a day off school. Well, you can have a snow day whenever you like on ROBLOX! Dive into some super snowy games and wrap up against the cold as you ski, slide down hills, chuck snowballs and mess about in the white stuff. Invite your friends and have a snow day to remember... even in the middle of summer!

SNOW RESORT

GAMES TO PLAY
- SNOW RESORT
- SNOWMAN SIMULATOR

96 JOIN A HANG OUT

TOP TIP!
In Guilty, you can create custom questions for your friends to answer.

'Hang out' games are when the whole group in a lobby or all the players on a server join together to make gameplay decisions, usually in a quirky contest or fun battle. They can be based around 'a or b' type questions, such as in Would You Rather...? or Would You Quiz, and you get to see if you can put a winning run together. Give Guilty a try too, and play with your friends for a chilled hang out experience!

Who's most likely to cover their eyes during a horror movie?

GUILTY

GAMES TO PLAY
- GUILTY
- WOULD YOU QUIZ?

97 BE READY TO RESET

If things aren't going your way or your avatar is in trouble, the reset function can be a lifesaver. You may have a fault with a game or be stuck on a level, for example, and you don't want to quit the game entirely. Selecting the Restart Character option will return you to a spawn point so you can then carry on. It's quick and easy, so don't worry about using it – resetting could soon set you off a winning streak.

Player 1 @Player1
Player 2 @Player2
Player 3 @Player1
Player 4 @Player1
Your Avatar @Your Avatar

R Reset Character   L Leave   ESC

TOP TIP!
Reset Character option is also next to the Leave Game quick exit button.

98 GET TIME REWARDS

SHINDO

Spending ages playing ROBLOX is easy for most gamers, and in some games there are rewards for the time you spend on screen! As an incentive to keep playing and progressing, it's often possible to collect cool items and unlock extras based on the time you put in. Lucky Blocks Battlegrounds offers up super blocks after 15 minutes of play, diamond blocks for those playing more than 30 minutes.

GAMES TO PLAY

- LUCKY BLOCKS BATTLEGROUNDS
- SHINDO

99 BE A DJ

FUN FACT!
Alexnewtron, the amazing developer behind MeepCity, also released a cool music game called Club DJ.

With music and sound enabled, now is your chance to show the ROBLOX world your DJ skills. You don't need to be a music master – just pick a bangin' game with loads of choices, then have fun mixing the beats and vocals. Splash Music is one of the best at this. With genres of music such as dance, hip hop and rock, plus all the tech and buttons ready to spin some slick tunes, you'll look and sound like a pro in no time.

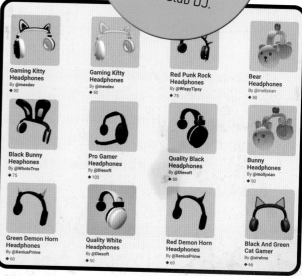

Gaming Kitty Headphones
By @mexdev
◆ 50

Gaming Kitty Headphones
By @mexdev
◆ 50

Red Punk Rock Headphones
By @WispyTipsy
◆ 75

Bear Headphones
By @mollyxian
◆ 50

Black Bunny Heaphones
By @WhotoTrus
◆ 75

Pro Gamer Headphones
By @Diesoft
◆ 100

Quality Black Headphones
By @Diesoft
◆ 50

Bunny Headphones
By @mollyxian
◆ 50

Green Demon Horn Headphones
By @XeniusPrime
◆ 60

Quality White Headphones
By @Diesoft
◆ 50

Red Demon Horn Headphones
By @XeniusPrime
◆ 60

Black And Green Cat Gamer
By @sirehns
◆ 66

100 GO TO SPACE

FUN FACT!
If you want a tough space challenge, in Olympus Mons you're faced with climbing the tallest mountain on Mars.

Enjoy a ROBLOX adventure that's absolutely out of this world! All types of players love taking an intergalactic trip, hopping on a rocket or a spaceship and zooming to new dimensions. Choose between a range of space-themed titles that either build a spacecraft and equipment, navigate missions from Earth or tackle alien invaders. Ride a Rocket to the Space Station and Moon may be a long game title, but this clever classic from 2010 is always good fun!

RIDE A ROCKET

GAMES TO PLAY
- SPACE SAILORS
- SPACE COMBAT TYCOON
- RIDE A ROCKET TO THE SPACE STATION AND MOON

(101) HAVE FUN!

Yep – ROBLOX is 100 per cent about enjoying yourself! The platform was created in 2006 as a fun and unique place for players across the globe to come together and enjoy a crazy collection of activities. The thousands of games to choose from all have one thing in common, and that's to entertain and make us come back again and again to play them. Even if you're being chased by a monster, battling an enemy or leaping across obstacles, in ROBLOX you'll always have a smile on your face!

How will your gameplay take shape? YOU decide.

The best ROBLOX players never miss an opportunity and enjoy every moment.